A Little Book for
Preachers

101 Ideas for Better Sermons

James E. Miller

Augsburg
MINNEAPOLIS

To Christen, with respect as well as love.

A LITTLE BOOK FOR PREACHERS
101 Ideas for Better Sermons

Illustrations are from the Dover Pictorial Archive Series.

Library of Congress Cataloging-in-Publication Data

Miller, James E., 1945-
    A little book for preachers : 101 ideas for better sermons / by James E. Miller ; foreword by Nancy R. Faus.
      p. cm.
    ISBN 0-8066-2991-6 (alk. paper)
    1. Preaching. I. Title.
BV4211.2.M52 1996   96-22267
251—dc20   CIP

The paper used in this publication meets the minimum requirements of American National Standard for Information Sciences—Permanence of Paper for Printed Library Materials, ANSI Z329.48-1984.   ♾

Manufactured in the U.S.A.   AF 9-2991

00	99	98	97	96	1	2	3	4	5	6	7	8	9	10

Foreword

There's so much more to sermon planning than meets the eye. Creating powerful messages and preaching them effectively takes study, crafting, practice, and prayer. Jim Miller's practical, down-to-earth suggestions offer fresh insights into each step of the preaching process. His book is filled with ideas that will make even the best preacher say, "Why didn't I think of that?" and remind us all of the awesome responsibility we have whenever we step into the pulpit.

This book is not only for the first-time preacher; it provides lecture food for introductory preaching courses and a source of invaluable tips for the experienced pastor's bookshelf. Preaching is a storyteller's art—the art of telling God's marvelous, life-changing story that becomes our story. Jim Miller's 101 ideas can help the storyteller perfect that art and find energy and passion to proclaim the good news of Jesus Christ in new and exciting ways.

NANCY R. FAUS
BRIGHTBILL PROFESSOR OF MINISTRY STUDIES
BETHANY THEOLOGICAL SEMINARY

A Word from the Author

July 2, 1995

Christen,

I never imagined I would write these words. I am no longer a preacher. I no longer undergo those weekly sermon rituals that were once such an important part of my life. What do I have to say about preaching anymore?

Then a few months ago you said, "Dad, there's something I want to talk to you about." And you spoke an unexpected word: "seminary."

That was not a dream I ever held for you. Yet something within me quickens as I think about this step you're taking. Something within me sings as I think about you preaching your first sermon. And something within me wants to do the fatherly thing and the preacherly thing—namely, give you some advice.

There are a few things I wish people had said to me when I was first begin-ning to preach: simple suggestions that would have saved me discomfort, labor, and grief. There are simple procedures that would have helped me be a better preacher at an earlier age.

So I'll offer you what I wish someone had taken the time to offer me. Some of these suggestions should never be ignored; they are universal and unchanging. Some, on the other hand, deserve to be disregarded, and perhaps often. You'll have to figure out for yourself which are which.

Use these ideas however you will. I offer them with the knowledge you and I are not the same. But I also offer them with the awareness that a part of me flows through you in some mysterious way. And it is for that part that I write.

Love,
Dad

I wrote those words the day before my twenty-three-year-old daughter preached her first sermon the summer before she left for seminary. I also wrote down sixty-three suggestions in the form of a little book. After her sermon, I gave the book to her as a gift, along with the Bible my bishop gave me when I was ordained.

My little book passed from hand to hand until one day it occurred that Christen's book was perhaps for someone other than her. The number of ideas was enlarged, the personal statements eliminated, and the text was rewritten for men as well as women. The result is what you hold in your hands. It is no longer Christen's book—it is yours.

JIM MILLER
FORT WAYNE, INDIANA

PART ONE

Preparing the Preacher

1. Build a library.

Yes, sermons sometimes find their own way to you. But almost always you must do some digging. One of the best places to dig is a library— one that's no farther away than the end of your arm. Here are some essentials for starting a personal library: at least three Bible translations in addition to your favorite, including one that contains the Apocrypha; several commentaries; a Greek lexicon; reference books about life in biblical times; a large dictionary; a thesaurus; an almanac; and several books of quotations and anecdotes. Build your library each year. Make it reflect your tastes. And let it enrich your sermons.

2. Read all you can. Then read some more.

Read a couple of newspapers daily, including one from out of town. Comb a newsmagazine each week. Dip into several other magazines regularly. Subscribe to at least one professional journal. Read biographies and autobiographies to collect valuable life lessons and interesting anecdotes. Read fiction to see all the wonderful ways words can work together. Try poetry. Read things that have nothing to do with preaching. You'll soon discover that everything has to do with preaching.

3. Keep writing tools near at hand.

You can never tell when you'll hear a great story. Or read a fascinating fact. Or hatch a terrific thought. Or see a wonderful sight. Whenever that happens, go for a pen or pencil, or—if you're a computer geek—a keyboard. Jot notes in your appointment book. Or carry a small notebook in your purse or pocket or briefcase. Keep a pad of paper next to your bed at night. Find ways to preserve these little pearls throughout the day and night. Don't say, "I'll remember it later." You won't—at least not with the enthusiasm and insight you first had.

4. Build a file of anecdotes and quotations.

Good anecdotes and quotations make your sermons more interesting, concrete, and memorable. Start your own file system. For years the most reliable method has been file cards. Put only one story, example, or quotation on each card and indicate its source. Or use a computer data base program. File each item under a topic, like "perseverance," "forgiveness," or "children." File an entry under two or three headings if it's appropriate, so you don't have to cross-reference. Make a note on the card each time you use it so you won't repeat it too soon.

5. *Keep files of general information by topic.*

These will provide you with background information, general facts and figures, and notes on a host of subjects. Use manila file folders. Drop in whatever suits your fancy: newspaper stories, magazine articles, transcripts of TV programs, photocopied pages from books, pamphlets that cross your desk. Collect sermons or lectures, notes from seminars, and suggestions of resources. Here's the rule of thumb: "If in doubt, save it."

6. Let others help you gather files.

Up-to-date and easy-to-use files require ongoing work. Might a secretary handle sorting and typing for you? Would a volunteer in your congregation make this their ministry—a retired librarian, or someone who's an avid reader? Make sure this person understands what you want to save and how you wish it stored. In an occasional sermon, refer to someone supplying a helpful story or excerpt from their reading. That's a go-ahead for others to do the same. Your sermons will be more stimulating, people in your congregation will feel validated, and your job will be easier.

7. *Stay current.*

German theologian Karl Barth advised every preacher to go into the pulpit with the Bible in one hand and a newspaper in the other. Nowadays two hands aren't enough—you need to be outfitted with a backpack and wired for electricity. Watch television so you know what people are watching. Screen current movies, attend plays, rent videos. Whether or not you've made your peace with computers, you need to know what software is doing and where the Internet is heading and what satellites are sending. Sure, it's a task, but it's critically important. And it can be fun!

8. Keep a journal.

It's one thing to stay in touch with writers and speakers. It's an altogether different thing to stay in touch with yourself. But if you cannot do that, you cannot preach effectively. The way to know another is to know yourself. A good way to monitor your thoughts and feelings is by writing in a journal. Write every day or even several times a day. Write about your joys and frustrations, your fears and hopes, your opinions and reflections. Hardly any of this writing will make it into your sermons. But your sermons will still be the better for it. And so will you.

9. *Learn from the pros.*

Sit at the feet of that wonderful preacher named Jesus of Nazareth. Pay close attention, not just to what he said, but how he said it. Then study preachers who came afterward: Paul and Origen, John Chrysostom and Bernard of Clairvoux, Augustine and Aquinas. Read sermons by Luther, Calvin, Whitefield, and Wesley. See what Mary Savage, Sally Parsons, Sojourner Truth, and Lucretia Mott had to say. Familiarize yourself with the more recent words of Dwight Moody, Billy Sunday, Harry Emerson Fosdick, Paul Tillich, Georgia Harkness, Martin Luther King Jr., and Howard Thurman.

10. Learn from well-known contemporary preachers.

Expose yourself to some of today's effective preachers. Watch for a chance to hear men like Fred Craddock, John R. Stott, William Willimon, Walter Burghardt, Billy Graham, and Charles Swindoll. Experience the richness of African-American preaching through individuals like Gardner Taylor, Ella Pearson Mitchell, Cynthia Hale, and James Forbes. Listen for the unique voice women bring to the pulpit through the preaching of Barbara Brown Taylor, Edwina Hunter, Barbara Lundblad, and Barbara B. Zikmund.

11. Learn from lesser-known preachers.

The grapevine will tell you who's doing solid preaching in your area. Get to know those people. Attend their worship services when you can manage it. Participate in joint community services, or arrange pulpit exchanges. Form a small group of fellow preachers and study together. Critique one another. Collaborate. Help one another grow.

12. Study good books about preaching.

Homiletics is an evolving discipline as well as an art. Read some of the latest books on homiletics:

The Practice of Preaching by Paul Wilson
Preaching Through the Christian Year by Fred Craddock
The Preaching Life by Barbara B. Taylor
Preaching Liberation by James H. Harris
Black Preaching by Henry H. Mitchell
Preaching & the Literary Forms of the Bible by Thomas G. Long

13. Listen. Listen again. Listen some more.

There's only one way to know what people in your congregation are searching for, what they're afraid of, what they're drawn to. That's to listen to them. One of the greatest gifts you can give another is to listen to them well enough and long enough so that you can allow your voice to express their voice. So listen in living rooms and in offices, at bedsides and over lunch tables. Listen to individuals and families, to the young and the wise, the frivolous and the serious. *Really* listen.

14. Lead a full life.

If you consider yourself only a preacher, you cannot be much of a preacher. For the act of preaching is much more than standing before a group of people on Sunday morning. Your preaching must be grounded first of all in the Word of God. But it must also arise from who you are as a person. Your words must emerge from your experiences. Your Sabbath day speaking must carry with it all the other days of the week. For your words to give life, they must grow out of your deep experience of living. And dying. And being born again.

15. *Maintain a life of the soul.*

Sometimes preachers are so busy caring for other people's souls, they neglect their own. You cannot truly pray for others unless you are grounded in your own life of prayer. So set aside plenty of time to pray, to read devotions, to meditate on the Word. Create times of solitude that cannot be interrupted. Make pilgrimages. Take retreats. Cultivate a spiritual friendship with another, or place yourself in the care of a spiritual director. Treat this part of your life for what it is: sacred.

16. Plan your strategy far in advance.

Preaching is much too important to be left to your whims. You cannot say all that begs to be said by planning ahead a week or a month at a time. You need a longer view. Will you let the lectionary guide you through the year? Will you create topical sermons, either week by week or season by season? Or will you experiment with a combination of the two? Plan at least six months ahead. Devote several days to long-range planning. Get away by yourself, so you're not distracted. But remember: once in a while something happens that calls for your careful planning to be set aside. Sometimes plans are made by Another.

17. *Study scripture texts in a systematic fashion.*

Your preaching must flow from Scripture. It doesn't work if you use Scripture merely to shore up what you wish to say. You must place yourself at Scripture's feet and learn. A good way to do that is with a group—weekly meetings with a cadre of clergy, or with laypeople. Begin working with texts several weeks before you preach from them. Study the meaning of words and phrases. Uncover cultural contexts. Be open to what you may discover. You'll be rewarded in your search and strengthened for your task.

18. Create a file for every upcoming sermon.

Use manila folders to create your second filing system: ideas for each sermon or sermon series. Watch for helpful quotations, articles, and book chapters. Make notes about conversations you've had, songs you've heard, movies you've seen, stories you've come upon, current events that have moved you. Commit your reflections to paper and drop them in the file with everything else. Gather five times what you need. Then you'll be able to offer, not what you've gleaned, but what you've sifted.

19. Be true to your gender.

As you prepare yourself and your sermon material, be faithful to the way God has created you. Whether you're female or male, approach your preaching in a way that acknowledges and affirms your God-given abilities and strengths. And whether you're male or female, affirm the ways the other sex goes about the task of preaching and learn from them.

20. Be true to yourself.

You may be shy by nature, or gregarious. You may be methodical, or intuitive. Or both. Or neither. Whoever you are, you are not meant to deny your basic self as you prepare to preach. Some folks are naturally flamboyant in their sermons, while others communicate effectively in a no-nonsense manner. Some people preach with lots of volume, while others preach just as loudly with a quiet voice. Remember that God could speak equally well through a tongue-tied Moses and an eloquent Aaron, through an intense Martha and a reflective Mary. You are called to be *fully* who you are. You are called to be real.

21. Remember: it's dumb to appear too smart.

Just because you understand some Greek doesn't mean everyone needs to know it. Or wants to know. Just because you know how to pronounce long theological words doesn't mean you should spew them from the pulpit. Illustrations that are too erudite can separate you from your listeners. Never try to impress with your knowledge. In fact, don't try to impress with anything. Just do what you can to be clear, true, and honest.

22. *Never underestimate your audience.*

People who gather around you in worship have been exposed to thousands of professional presentations. They've listened to radio broadcasts, concerts, audiotapes, compact discs. They've watched award-winning television programs interspersed with glitzy advertisements. They've learned to gauge speakers quickly. They will sense if you believe what you say and if you know what you're talking about. However sharp you are, they're sharper.

23. Do the perfect thing: make some mistakes.

One of the biggest mistakes you can make is to try not to make any mistakes. However hard you work at doing everything right, sometimes you'll say the wrong word or make the wrong move. You're only human. And it's precisely your humanity that makes you approachable and believable. So relax and be natural. Your goofs will also signal an important truth: there is a limit to your dependability. No one should ever put their entire trust in you. There is only One worthy of such trust.

24. Accept the limits of your preaching.

A sermon is a powerful medium. It can bring alive the Word of God for a particular people in a particular place at a particular time. But there is much a sermon cannot do. It cannot say everything. It cannot reach all people in the same way. On their own, your words cannot change people, or change relationships, or change the world. You cannot make everything right. There will always be a powerlessness to your preaching, however powerful your sermons might be.

25. *Allow yourself to be guided.*

A sermon of truth and authority may come *through* you, but it does not come just *from* you. Sometimes, in fact, you will be called upon simply to stay out of the sermon's way. You may find yourself being steered to say what you didn't expect to say, or what you didn't want to say. It's then you come to remember that it's God who is guiding, as only God can. You're in this together.

PART TWO

Preparing the Sermon

26. *Do your own exegesis first.*

The only way to understand what a biblical text says is to figure it out. So uncover the meanings of Aramaic and Greek and Hebrew words for yourself. Learn all you can about specific biblical events and about all the players involved. Go into each passage with eyes as fresh as possible. Turn to commentaries only after that passage has come alive for you. Except in rare cases, don't refer to your work of exegesis in the sermon. When an artist unveils her painting, does she describe how she achieved its colors?

27. Brood.

Take plenty of time to ruminate on your text. Ponder ideas for your sermon as they come to you. Toy with them. Reorder them. Simplify them. Let your mind wander as you walk or run or drive. Let your thoughts ramble in the kitchen or in the shower or in the woods. Sleep on your ideas. Meditate on them. Pray over them. You cannot rush a fine sermon.

28. *Find your most creative time, then use it.*

Do your sermon planning and writing when you're the most productive. For many, that's in the morning. For others, fertile times appear at different hours. Discover your own rhythms and take advantage of them. Give yourself whatever private time you need. A sermon is too important to be given anything less than your full energy and creativity.

29. Create an outline before you begin writing.

You dare not bypass this critical step, no matter how confident you feel. List your main points in order. Note what you'll include in each. Plot what you'll say at the beginning of your sermon and at the ending. Live with your outline a while. Does it hang together? Does it flow? Does it build? Does it convince? When you're comfortable with your plan, follow its lead. Sometimes, once your outline is complete, the sermon will write itself.

30. Write your sermon.

"But I don't use a manuscript on Sunday morning," you may say. No matter—write one out anyway. Writing your sermon word for word forces you to sharpen and refine it. It leads you to become more clear about which thoughts communicate best, which words sound best, which transitions move best. It encourages you to be concrete and practical. It helps you see if parts of your sermon are too long or too short. Writing your sermon will help you improve as a speaker, whether or not you take your manuscript into the pulpit.

31. Condense your message into a single sentence.

If you cannot state your sermon's theme in one simple sentence, you're trying to say too much or you're not sure what you're trying to say. Either way, you're courting disaster. Before you write a word of your sermon, distill its basic idea down to ten or twelve words. Write these on a notecard. Keep going back to that card as you prepare your sermon. When you're finished, underline the kernel sentence that summarizes the sermon's basic idea. If you cannot find that thought in your sermon, how can you expect your listeners to?

32. Write simply.

Use language people understand. Write short sentences. Choose concrete words, active verbs. Avoid too many adjectives and adverbs—they get in the way of aural communication. Make it easy for people to follow you. When your preaching is done, your listeners should be more aware of what you have said than how you said it.

33. Edit your words ruthlessly.

Even if you set out to write simply, you'll use words you don't need. You'll fall back on expressions that get in the way. You'll compose thoughts that are almost right, but not quite. Editing your words is one of the hardest things you'll have to do as a sermon writer. It's difficult to let go of something you've polished so well. But if it doesn't advance your message, you must cut it out. Remember George Bernard Shaw's apology to a friend: "I'm sorry it's such a long letter—I didn't have time to write a short one."

34. *Write for the ear, not the eye.*

Write your sermon to be heard, not read. Listen to how most of us speak, then imitate that style. Use contractions like "it's" and "won't." Choose words that are easy to pronounce. Sometimes employ incomplete sentences. Use personal pronouns like "you" and "we" and "our." They reach out to embrace your audience. Stop from time to time as you write your sermon and read it aloud. Does it sound like you're talking to a friend? If not, try again.

35. Use fresh, clear language.

Employ words with great care. Watch your grammar. Check for correct definitions. Make it your goal, not to find unusual words to use, but to use usual words in fresh ways. Choose words that are rich in meaning and clear in content. Be on the lookout for language that can speak to the mind, heart, and soul simultaneously. Always cultivate an abiding appreciation for the magic of words.

36. Write to engage the mind.

People tire of listening. They can think much faster than they can hear words. So they tend to "wander off," sometimes amplifying the speaker's thoughts, sometimes dialoguing with them, sometimes ignoring them entirely. Preachers must continually gather and re-gather the minds of listeners. How do you do that? Voice questions people are asking themselves, and then answer them. Use words and phrases that create pictures. Pepper your sermons with illustrations. Design the sermon to build to a climax.

37. *Write to engage the heart and soul.*

Once your listeners' minds are engaged, you must engage their hearts and souls as well. Some of the ideas you present are suited only for the head. But your sermon won't come alive for people unless you touch their feelings and yearnings too. You can do that with the stories you tell, the memories you invoke, the relationships you call upon, the beckonings you give voice to. Truly effective sermons appeal to the mind and the heart and the soul in equal measure.

38. Hook your listeners' attention immediately.

You have only thirty seconds in which to get your congregation thinking, "This could be interesting. I think I'll listen." Open with the unpredictable. Ask a provocative question. Recite an interesting quotation. State a startling fact. Offer well-timed humor that leads into your main point. Once your listeners are with you, move ahead. Let your opening indicate what's in store for them, then deliver what you say you will.

39. End with flair.

Despite advice to the contrary, it's not always wise to end a sermon by telling your listeners what you've already told them. If you've done your job well, they don't need reminding. They simply need a channeling of their energy. End with a little "zinger." Or repeat that unifying quote. Or give examples of what the listeners can do. Your congregation will appreciate fair warning you're about to end. Put them on notice, and then move briskly to your conclusion. All things being equal, people will remember two parts of your sermon: what they first heard and what they last heard. Give them something worth remembering.

40. Keep quotations short.

Listeners cannot "fast forward" to the end of a thought, nor can they push "rewind" to replay it. Read or recite quotations that do not overtax people's ability to follow. A few lines of poetry or prose or thirty to sixty seconds of recitation is all most people can follow with ease. When you identify the source of your quotation, keep details to a minimum. But make sure the author receives full credit lest you be accused of plagiarizing.

41. Tell stories.

People love stories. Retell Bible stories in your own words and in your own style as a way to breathe new life into them. Tell about things that happened to people recently and long ago. The best stories are often taken from real life, about people who really lived and struggled and persevered and died. Create scenes with your words. Include dialogue to add immediacy and personality. And always remember: sometimes the best life story comes from your own life.

42. Help your stories do their job.

Select your stories with care, making sure they arouse the feelings you want. Don't use too many anecdotes; they should take up no more than 10 percent of your sermon. Tell each story by itself; if you place two together, they lose effectiveness. Depending on your congregation and sermon, use stories that relate to sports, business, entertainment, prominent citizens, ordinary people, local news, national events. Sometimes a single story is all parishioners take home with them. Will you give them a story that does your sermon justice?

43. *Sometimes let a whole sermon be a story.*

Don't do this often. But every once in a while, weave a wonderful tale with a storyteller's art. Build scenes and episodes with which people can identify. Give personality to your characters. Change your voice to play the different roles. Act out your story. Invite others to share in the telling, after rehearsing it thoroughly. Tell your story well, then be seated. Let the story explain itself. If it's good, it will do so better than you ever could.

44. *Be creative with your sermon title, but not cute.*

Choose a title that will tell people the subject of your sermon rather than make them guess. Get their attention, but don't leave them laughing in the aisle. Or gagging. Remember that your sermon begins the moment they're introduced to it by its title. Make it a friendly introduction.

45. *Employ illustrations from and for both genders.*

Go back over the illustrations you've used in the past. Are lives of women represented equally with the lives of men? What about stories from the Bible that feature women and girls? Do your people know Sarah, Hannah, Esther, Miriam, Mary Magdalene, Priscilla, and their sisters? Be careful not to stereotype either sex. But be sure that your sermons speak clearly and equally to the women and the men in your audience.

46. Remember who's sitting in your pews.

Take Mother's Day, for example. Remember, some of your listeners don't have mothers any longer, and some never knew them. Some may have mothers who neglected or abused them. Others may have "mothers" who are grandmothers or older siblings or fathers. Keep in mind the single and divorced and widowed, as well as the married; the chronically ill and the dying, as well as those related to them; the gay and lesbian; those who are addicted and those who don't understand addiction. If you cannot adequately address a particular group's needs this week, perhaps you can next week. That's one of the beauties of being a preacher.

47. Preach to individuals.

Put the names of several people from your congregation on a notecard and let your eyes fall on those names from time to time as you prepare your sermon. Ask yourself, "Will she understand this?" "Do these words address issues he now faces?" It matters not whether those people are there when you preach the sermon. Others will know you have written that sermon expressly for each of them. They'll realize you're concerned about people, no matter what the topic of your sermon is. And what's more, they'll be right.

48. Be vulnerable.

A sermon is a good time to loosen your defenses a bit. Let people know who you are. Over time, tell them something of the struggles you've known, the joys you've felt. Model what it means to be open and growing. You can overdo this, of course. So don't hang out your dirty laundry for all to see. And don't share so much of your pain that your listeners cannot tap into their own. Just reveal enough so people will understand you better. Then lead them from your life into their lives, and into all of life.

49. Use humor.

People like to laugh. And it helps when they *do* laugh. Laughter creates bonds among listeners and with the speaker. It releases healing chemicals called endorphins into the bloodstream. Research indicates humor helps people assimilate information faster and retain it longer. So don't be afraid to joke. Jesus certainly wasn't. Can you imagine him talking about a lunker of a camel squeezing through the eye of a tiny needle with a straight face? Try using self-effacing humor. It makes you more human, more believable. So go ahead: have some fun.

50. Use humor appropriately.

Humor can serve you well as you introduce your sermon. It can help you illustrate human foibles, or underscore a reaction everyone understands, or a validate a feeling most people share. But just because you've found a joke that's innocent and funny doesn't mean it should be told. Each piece of humor must have a point and must relate to the flow of your message. If it doesn't, it will interrupt your audience's train of thought and distract them.

51. Include important late-breaking events in worship.

Sometimes critical things happen within your congregation or community in the days or hours just before you preach. When events conspire to alarm or enthrall your people, you have a responsibility and an opportunity to address those events. Try to work something into your sermon or pastoral announcements. Validate the importance of what has happened and the naturalness of people's feelings. Place these happening in a context of faith and the message of God in Christ.

52. Make it easy for people to follow you.

Repeating a short statement at intervals can pull people into your thought process. Read or listen to Martin Luther King's "I Have A Dream" speech and see how forcefully repetition can work. Your sermons can do the same thing for your parishioners. Other ways to escort your listeners include short reminders that identify the point you're making, or transitions that mark your place while signaling a change up ahead. But don't become so predictable with your patterns that listeners can easily rush on ahead of you. Come sermon time at least, expect them to follow you.

53. Don't try to imitate someone else.

Most clergy carry the memory of a preacher who especially influenced how they compose and present sermons. But trying to imitate another person in the pulpit is a sure recipe for failure. The act of preaching draws much of its authenticity and power from the uniqueness of one's personality and personal encounters with God and the world. There is a sense in which preaching is not something you do—it's something you are. And you cannot be yourself if you're imitating another.

54. Preach humbly.

Some preachers take great pride in what they do. The act of standing before a receptive group of people lends itself to that feeling. But honest preaching is humbling. You must ask yourself Sunday after Sunday, "What right do I have to speak with authority on this subject, given who I am and what I have done?" Preaching is not something you *deserve* to do; it's something you're *allowed* to do. Preaching with humility makes you a better person and a better Christian as well as a better preacher.

55. Preach to yourself. Always.

Preaching dare not be something you do only for other people. Your preaching is for you, too. Always start with yourself and never leave yourself. When you speak the truth as you know it, apply it to yourself first and last. When you speak of sin, keep in mind your own. When you speak of salvation, remember your own need and your own experience. When you speak of love, inwardly acknowledge what a miser you can be, and sometimes what a dear.

56. *Never exploit people's emotions.*

Each time you preach you're given a rare entrée into people's lives. You're offered latitude to say what you want in the way you want. But be ever so cautious when you evoke people's feelings. You have the power to sway others by the fears you arouse, by the anger you feed, by the helplessness you engender, by the adoration you encourage. Your hold on people is real. Remember how much people will trust you. Make your preaching—and all of your ministry—worthy of that trust.

57. Avoid moralizing.

Preachers moralize in different ways. Some deliver hard and fast rules that are not to be broken. Others are more subtle; they overuse words like "always" and "never," "good" and "bad." They're heavy with their "shoulds." A healthier and more effective way is to preach the Word with humility and compassion. Then your listeners can interact with that Word themselves, letting it bring light to their lives. When the "shoulds" come out of their own wrestling with what's moral and what's not, people become more responsible personally and more mature ethically.

58. *Beware of projecting.*

It's a universal human phenomenon to place upon others what we don't wish to see in ourselves. It's easier to handle what we don't like about ourselves from that safe distance. But it's also dangerous. Be honest enough to regularly ask yourself questions like these: "What do I not like seeing within myself?" "What do I feel compelled to hide about myself?" It's painful to look at this darker side of yourself. But it hurts even more when you don't. For then you run the risk of making others out to be what they're not. And you allow yourself to be less than you could be: a whole person.

59. Empower your listeners.

Your best sermons will lead parishioners to become more than mere listeners. Your preaching will make people both think and feel while you speak, and then lead them to do more of each once you sit down. Ideally, the process won't stop there. People will be equipped to proclaim the Gospel themselves to a world crying for that message. Ideally, your preaching will vitalize and mobilize your listeners, preparing them to do what they alone can do. Truth is, they can do ever so much more than you.

60. Never treat a children's sermon as "only a children's sermon."

Treat it as a significant, timely message for some important, curious, unusually open human beings who happen to be children. Speak in language appropriate to them, but never talk down to them. Have fun with them but never do so at their expense. Put yourself on their level in as many ways as you can—physically, emotionally, and spiritually. You'll find if you give this the time and energy and attention it deserves, the children will lift you up to their level.

61. Practice your sermon.

The stakes are too high to leave your sermon delivery to chance. Your moments before people are too limited, your message too important. So after you've written your sermon, rehearse it. Speak into a tape recorder. Even better, go to the place you'll preach and deliver the sermon beforehand all by yourself. Experiment with intonation and gesturing. Practice one last time as close to the hour of worship as possible. Then you'll be comfortable with what you have to say and excited about saying it.

62. Prepare your manuscript for easy use.

If you take your complete manuscript into the pulpit, make it effortless to use. See that it's typed or printed out. For easy reading, use serif rather than sans serif type, upper and lower case, and double spacing. Allow enough margin to make notes to yourself: "Go slow here." "Emphasize this." Leave the bottom two inches of your pages empty so your eyes aren't drawn too low. "Dog-ear" the upper corner of each sheet so you can slip it to one side with ease. Number your pages at the top. Underline key words in a different color. Never, never read your sermon. Know it well enough so you can tell it, even if you're following your manuscript word for word.

PART THREE

Preparing for Worship

63. *Carve out a time of quiet beforehand.*

Often you're bombarded with last-minute particulars right before worship: signals to check, announcements to note, people to greet. In order to deal calmly with all these details and your upcoming sermon too, it will help if you are quieted within. Spend time alone in whatever cozy space will give you privacy. Do any of these: perform relaxation exercises, listen to soothing music, sit in silence, meditate and pray. Gather yourself together and gather yourself to God.

64. Dress comfortably.

So often it's little things that make a big difference. Wear comfortable shoes into the worship service. It's more tiring to stand there than most people think. Choose clothing that lets you move with ease and clothing that breathes. You'll perspire more than usual. Select attire that helps you feel confident. If you're ill-at-ease with your appearance, you're more likely to be distracted as you preach. You will communicate much more than you realize before you ever say a word.

65. Dress comfortably for others.

What you wear and how you wear it affects others. Bold patterns can be dizzying, especially if you move around much. Colors that are too extreme will clamor for attention. Dancing earrings and noisy bracelets can be bothersome. Empty your pockets of all potentially distracting coins and keys. Hairstyles should not hide too much of your face or demand too much of your hands. Beards and mustaches should be carefully trimmed around the mouth. Contact lenses are the best eyewear, but full-size glasses with an anti-glare coating will work. Avoid half-frame reading glasses; the obvious eye movements such spectacles require can be very disconcerting.

66. *Remember your supplies.*

You never know when a thought will come to you before your sermon. Or when you'll want to jot down a name or date or task. So carry a pen into worship, but don't make its presence obvious. And don't have it anywhere near your hands while you preach. Facial tissue, cough drops, or throat lozenges can also be good traveling companions. Place a glass of water nearby and make sure it's not too cold. The closer to your body temperature the water is, the better it is for your vocal chords. Don't make a show of drinking it. Just use it if it will help you.

67. Don't be nervous about being nervous.

It's normal to feel nervous before an important public event. If you pay too much attention to your nervousness, you'll only increase it, inviting people to be nervous for you. And, nervousness is good for you. A moderate level of "the jitters" is a sign of how seriously you take your preaching. Your stress reaction activates your adrenaline supply, speeding up your mental activity. That's energy you can harness to sharpen your skill and focus your concentration. Should the time ever come when you go into the pulpit without feeling anxious, that will be something to be anxious about.

68. *Plan for your own worship needs.*

In addition to preparing yourself *before* worship, plan little ways to prepare yourself *during* worship. Consciously choose to become a vessel for God as you enter the sanctuary and as you rise to preach. Select hymns and music that lead *you* into the sermon and prayer along with your congregation. Allow for moments of silence that give room for the Spirit to move. By your own singing, listening, praying and being silent, you can participate fully in the service of worship yourself. The more you meet your own worship needs, the more you'll meet others'.

69. Fit the pulpit to you.

Create an environment in the pulpit that feels right to you. Of first importance: don't let the pulpit swallow you up. People want to see more than the tops of your shoulders and your head. If you need, add a step or a box. Carpet it. Arrange to have your notes at the proper angle for your eyes. Make sure the lighting is good. Work with the microphone beforehand until it suits you. If you choose not to deliver your sermon from the pulpit, you might want to at least start there. The pulpit is an important symbol of tradition and strength.

70. Exude energy.

This may come naturally to you, or you may need to prime yourself. People in the pews want to feel your presence and your vitality. They want to sense your passion. The only way they'll know it is if you show it. Don't amble to the pulpit. Stride. Don't slouch in the pulpit. Stand tall. Release yourself. Take flight. Soar.

PART FOUR

Preaching the Sermon

71. *Approach preaching as high adventure.*

Preaching is not for the fainthearted. It's for the daring, for the ones who are not afraid to stand up and say what they believe—and for those who are afraid and stand up anyway. Effective preaching contains an element of high drama. All the hours of listening, reading, pondering, praying, and writing come down to a few moments of unpredictability. What will happen during the sermon? Will people hear? Will God's Word be communicated? You can never tell. All you can do is prepare fully and then preach bravely. The rest is in Someone Else's hands.

72. *Take command as you begin.*

It's hard to overestimate the importance of your sermon's beginning. More than anything, your listeners want you to take charge and to succeed. Build on the positive anticipation they bring. Take your time as you ready yourself, as you look directly into their faces, as you take your first breath. Give yourself five or ten seconds to do this. Then start speaking with confidence, authority, and feeling. If you use a manuscript, commit the first thirty seconds of your sermon to memory so you won't have to break eye contact.

73. *Realize that your words need help.*

Research proves what preachers don't always like to hear: 60 percent or more of spoken communication rests with the nonverbals. The ideas, the images, and the language all count. But what counts even more is the tone of the voice, the look in the eye, the gesture of the hand, the expression on the face. Even the most elevating words, when presented poorly in a monotone drone, will go nowhere. If your sermon is going to amount to anything, your words will need help.

74. Preach with your eyes.

If you really want to know someone, you look into their eyes. That's their most expressive part. Your eyes are critical to your preaching. Train yourself to make regular eye contact with people in every part of the sanctuary. Move your eyes purposefully about the room and look at individuals several seconds at a time. Move from person to person as you move from thought to thought. Never go more than ten seconds without looking up. Your eyes are your most direct link with your people. Use them for that.

75. Preach with your face.

Not everyone in your congregation will be able to see your eyes as well as they wish. So your face must augment your words. Be facile with your face, especially when you tell stories, express emotions, and make important points. A few things *don't* help. Ill-timed or fleeting facial expressions communicate insecurity. Frozen faces may signal fear or hostility. Or nothing at all. The human face has a natural repertoire of thousands of expressions. Coax a few to give your sermon depth and feeling.

76. *Project your voice.*

To preach well, you must be heard well. If your voice is too quiet, people will think you're doubtful or indecisive or uninterested. If you want to reach your audience, you must project. Projection has less to do with volume than energy. Launch your voice from deep within—from the muscles of your diaphragm, rather than from your neck and throat. Speak your words with your whole being. Thrust your sermon out. Give it life so it can give life.

77. *Preach naturally.*

The sound people most want to hear from you is your own voice. They'll be put off if you give it an especially pious ring. They'll feel duped if you try to sound like someone else. They'll be confused if your pulpit voice bears no resemblance to the one you use at their bedside or in their home. Relax your vocal chords. Speak in rhythms that sound like your natural phrasing. Use variety in your tone and speed. Pause for little intervals, just as you do in everyday speech. Sound like a conversationalist. Then you'll really be preaching.

78. *Preach clearly.*

Enunciate carefully. Concentrate on activating the lower half of your face: move your jaw, open your mouth fully, limber your lips, free your tongue. Watch out for utterances that muddy your speech: repeated sounds of "uh" and "er"; repetition of words like "well," "y'know," and "okay?". The overuse of pet phrases can cloud what you have to say. Then however clearly you're speaking, you're not speaking clearly.

79. *Preach with your hands and arms.*

A sermon without gestures is muffled. Learn to use your hands as you talk. Practice expressive motions that synchronize with your voice and your face as well as your words. It helps if these movements anticipate rather than follow your thoughts. Employ flowing gestures that move out from your body to include your listeners. Develop a variety of hand and arm motions to communicate different ideas. Remember that larger rooms and larger audiences call for larger gestures. Avoid nervous gestures such as hand wringing and palm rubbing, or clamping for dear life onto the sides of the pulpit.

80. Preach with your body.

Why stop with your head and arms and hands? Speak with your whole body! Place your feet firmly, about shoulder width apart, your weight equally distributed. Don't lock your knees. Shift your legs and feet from time to time. Turn your entire body to face different parts of the sanctuary. Avoid leaning back as you preach: it distances you from the very people you want to reach. If anything, lean *toward* your people. Reach out to them with your entire being.

81. Preach slowly and deliberately.

Speak more slowly than you think you ought, and chances are you'll be only a *little* too fast. Pause between thoughts. Give your questions time to sink in. Use these interludes as vocal underlines, as if you were saying, "Think about it." Remember that silence is a voice of God. It can fill spaces before and after you speak, within your prayers, and even as you enunciate. Be comfortable with an unhurried approach and short periods of silence, and your parishioners will listen better and remember longer.

82. Preach with conviction.

Noted preacher George Buttrick said that pulpit speech is closer to drama than to philosophy or logic. The sermon is vital enough that it deserves to bring out the thespian within every preacher. Do you get the impression Jesus spoke to the crowds as if he were reading lecture notes? Of course not. He pleaded and cajoled. He exhorted and proclaimed. He wove the most beguiling of stories. He wasn't afraid to captivate his audiences. Think about it. No, don't *think* about it. *Feel* it. *Do* it.

83. Preach to everyone.

Let no one in the sanctuary escape your gaze. Preach to youth as well as adults. Preach to your family as well as to strangers. Preach to those whom you know intimately as well as those you know only formally. Preach to those who share leadership of worship with you. And, of course, preach to yourself.

84. Ignore those who are sleeping.

It will probably happen every Sunday. Some people will be unusually tired. Some will have too much else going on in their lives. Some will be bored, either with or without good reason. You may be tempted to keep checking in with them, to see if you've captured their attention yet. That's like continually running your tongue across a tooth that's lost a filling. Concentrate on those who are with you. Everyone will be happier for your decision.

85. Draw on those who are expressive.

Some listeners have more expressive faces than others. Look at these people to see how well you're communicating, or if you are. Sometimes you may wish to draw energy from them. Don't overdo this or you'll end up preaching only to them. But from time to time they can be a source of strength and encouragement. These people will probably know when you're doing this, but you might tell them anyway and thank them for their role in your sermon.

86. If a baby or child is crying, let it be.

Don't look in consternation at the child or parent, much as you might be tempted. Just raise your speaking level slightly and proceed. Normally a parent or guardian will handle the situation quickly enough, even if you wish it could be more quickly. For those rare times when people are not sensitive, make sure your ushers quietly suggest "a temporary exit for the good of all concerned."

87. *If an adult is crying, let them be.*

But don't ignore them. Keep them in your gaze as much as ever, yet no more than is normal. Sometimes an extra touch on their arm or shoulder as you greet them afterward will communicate all you need and all they wish. Remember that people cry for all sorts of reasons. Tears of joy and gratitude can sometimes be mistaken for something else. And sometimes the tears that are falling have nothing to do with your words. Remember, too, that some people cry without showing it.

88. If the crying adult is you, let yourself be, too.

It may happen. If it does, you don't need to apologize. If you wish to say something in explanation, do so. Otherwise you need not make excuses. Just pause, breathe normally, gather yourself, and resume speaking. People will understand, and they will find their own ways of helping you as you continue preaching.

89. *Stretch your preaching.*

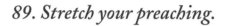

Whatever your age, experience, and abilities, try to stretch yourself every time you preach. The effort may be as simple as trying to be more spontaneous in the next four lines you've written. Or speak from notes rather than a manuscript. If you've never done so, deliver a sermon as a first-person story. If you've been tied to the pulpit, move away from it for part of a sermon. Go back to the pulpit if you've been away. Preach with fewer gestures and force your voice to make up the difference. Recite the entire scripture text by heart. Week by week, grow in your abilities.

90. *Stumble well.*

The pulpit is not a place for pratfalls. But it is a place where things can go wrong. It's a great place for tongues to get twisted and sentences to get forgotten and thoughts to get misplaced. When that happens, it's best to acknowledge and correct your mistake rather than pretend it never happened. Being able to do so with acceptance or even humor may communicate more than the text for the day.

91. Never apologize for your sermon.

Every clergyperson would like to preach an uninterrupted series of eloquent, memorable sermons. But some weeks the ideas won't come or the words won't flow. Some weeks your other duties will encroach on preparation time and you'll go into Sunday morning feeling unorganized and unready. As long as you've done all you could, go into the pulpit with your head held high. If your sermon is not up to snuff, people will know; but most of them will also admit this experience happens to everyone. And some people *won't* know, and they'll receive exactly what they've come to hear. God will use your words however God chooses.

92. *Don't overstay your welcome.*

Don't push your listeners beyond their limits. Time your sermon in advance so you know how long it will take. Keep your eye on a timepiece if that helps, but never lift your arm to look at your watch. Your listeners will do the same thing and you'll lose their attention. If you'd like your sermon to be talked about over Sunday dinner, make sure the subject will be something other than how interminable it seemed.

93. Exercise authority as you end.

Memorize the ending of your sermon as well as the beginning. Deliver it with your head up, your voice strong, your eyes connected to your listeners'. Speak each word so it's clearly understood. Slow your speed a bit. Pronounce your final words with a punch. Then stand frozen for a moment and let your words continue their journey inside your listeners. Don't be overly dramatic. Just be convincing and sure.

PART FIVE

Finishing the Process

94. Keep a record of every sermon.

Make notes on your manuscript after you've delivered a sermon. How did it go? What were its strengths? Which illustrations were most effective? What parts most captured people's interest? What would you have done differently? Someday go back through your file of sermons and notice how your preaching style is evolving. See what your preaching can tell you about your role, your faith, your God, even yourself.

95. *Get feedback on your sermon.*

You'll never know for sure how your sermon went unless you learn from other sources. Tape-record your message regularly. Then listen to it later in the week. Study your tone, inflection, pronunciation, and timing. Better yet, videotape your sermon. Study your eye movements, facial expressions, gestures, and other body language. Try watching with the sound turned off and learn even more. Ask someone you trust to give their evaluation. Will that person be your spouse? Absolutely not.

96. *Accept feedback graciously.*

When people greet you afterward, you'll often hear familiar comments: "Nice sermon, Pastor." "You gave me a lot to think about." Treat every comment with respect and grace. And keep your sense of humor. Keep in mind the preacher who had delivered his first sermon. A woman greeted him and said, "That was the worst sermon of all time." The minister was taken aback until the next person in line said, "Don't pay any attention to her, Pastor. She's always been a bit of a lunatic." The clergyman sighed in relief. "Yes," the person continued, "she just repeats what everyone else is saying."

97. *After your sermon has been delivered, let it go.*

It is no longer yours. It will mean whatever it will to whomever is touched by it. It will take on a life of its own, whether short or long, prominent or obscure. Kiss your sermon a sweet good-bye and send it off into the world. Trust that God will give it wings. Then watch it fly.

98. *Identify your preaching theme.*

Many preachers have a recurring theme to their sermons—one that grows out of their theology, life experiences, personality, understanding of ministry, and approach to preaching. Their sermons change titles, the scripture texts vary, yet a similar message keeps repeating itself. What are you like as a preacher? Are your sermons as full and varied as they could be?

99. *If you're an effective preacher, be careful.*

Every person who preaches has a lot at stake. But if you're a person who naturally commands attention by your preaching, if you're what's known as a "spellbinder," your stakes are even higher. Because people listen to you, you must make sure that what you offer is solid. Because people believe you, you must make sure what you say is true. Because people may idolize you, you must commit to preaching only the Gospel, only in humility, and only in love. Yours is an awesome responsibility.

100. Recognize the privilege that is yours.

You are entrusted with people's joys and hurts, theirs fears and hopes, their failures and strengths. You can say things no other professionals in our society can say. You are given a tremendous amount of freedom, respect, and trust, as well as plenty of acceptance, forgiveness, and love. Every time you preach, begin with a silent prayer of gratitude and end with a humble acknowledgment of grace. In between the two, do what you've been called to do. Preach the Word passionately.

101. Every time you preach, remember Whose the glory is.

The glory is God's. First of all. Last of all. Completely. And forever.

*This book could not have appeared as it has without Nancy Faus—
without her expert ideas, her gracious wisdom, her sensitive editing. She has
generously shared her accumulated knowledge about human communication,
her experience as a homiletics professor, and her skill as a first-rate preacher.
In the course of this project she has strengthened the areas in which I
have been weak and broadened my limited horizons time after time.
Without question, this is her book every bit as much as mine.*